Miracle
juices

A Pyramid Cooking Paperback

Miracle
juices

Charmaine Yabsley
and Amanda Cross

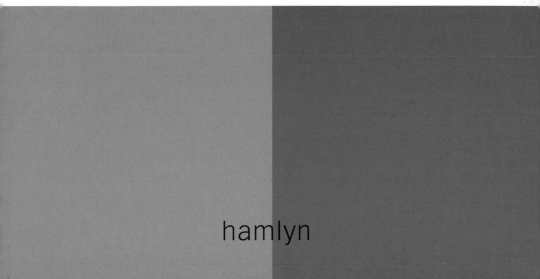

hamlyn

An Hachette UK Company
www.hachette.co.uk

A Pyramid Paperback

First published in Great Britain 2007 by Hamlyn,
a division of Octopus Publishing Group Ltd
Endeavour House, 189 Shaftesbury Avenue,
London WC2H 8JY
www.octopusbooks.co.uk
www.octopusbooksusa.com

This edition published in 2009

Distributed in the US by Hachette Book Group USA
237 Park Avenue, New York, NY 10017, USA

Distributed in Canada by Canadian Manda Group
165 Dufferin Street, Toronto, Ontario, Canada M6K 3H6

This material was previously published as *Miracle Juices*

ISBN 978-0-600-62029-7

A CIP catalogue record for this book is available from
the British Library

Printed and bound in China

10 9 8 7 6 5 4 3 2

All the recipes in this book have been tested using the
Oscar Pulverizing Juicer. If a different juicer is used, the
quantity of juice may vary.

Safety Note
This book should not be considered a replacement for
professional medical treatment; a physician should be
consulted on all matters relating to health. While the
advice and information in this book is believed to be
accurate, neither the author nor publisher can accept
any legal responsibility for any injury or illness sustained
while following the advice in this book.

contents

introduction

Feeling fit, healthy and energized is the ideal state for us all. But how often do we really feel on top of the world? Usually we're a little bit tired, feeling the beginnings of a cold, having trouble sleeping due to stress, or we just feel a bit run-down. While we tend to accept these symptoms as normal, we really shouldn't put up with anything less than 100 percent good health. Why should we have to try just to get through each day as opposed to living every moment to the full, with the interest and vigor to deal with each new situation and idea? This book has been devised for people who are dedicated to achieving and maintaining a healthy, holistic lifestyle, enjoying excellent health today while taking care of their tomorrows.

How juice can help

We all know we should eat at least five servings of fruit and vegetables each day to ensure that we maintain perfect health. However, with today's busy lifestyles, increased stress levels and exposure to pollution, more often than not we grab food on the run with little thought of its nutritional content and our daily requirements. Instead of regarding food as valuable fuel for our bodies, eating becomes merely another activity to perform each day. If your body was an automobile, you would put the best fuel into it and check it regularly to make sure its oil and water were topped up, wouldn't you? Yet many of us don't give our bodies the same amount of consideration, and tend to feed them whichever fuel is quick, easy and immediately available.

why juice?

Nutritional benefits

Fruit and vegetables are among the cheapest foods to buy and, in their raw state, require virtually no preparation. However, we still tend to reach for chips or cookies instead of carrots when we're hungry. Not only is there little nutritional value in junk or fast food, but we also tend to eat more of these foods in order to feel full. Understandably, eating a bag of apples or carrots is pretty hard going, and this is why juicing is so attractive. By pulping a bag of apples to create fresh apple juice, our bodies will receive a super boost of nutrients in an easily assimilated form and feel satisfied.

When it comes to fruit and vegetables, many of us overlook the nutritional benefits we can gain from making them into juices, and yet with a little effort you can juice your way to optimum health. Making your juice from good-quality produce guarantees a juice bursting with goodness. And, by combining several types of fruits and vegetables on a daily basis, you will ensure that your body receives its full quota of vitamins and minerals.

So what's the difference between making your own juice and buying it from the supermarket? Above all, the nutrients in fresh, homemade juice surpass anything you can buy. This is because the bought juice has been pre-squeezed and packaged and diluted with water, meaning the nutrients and health benefits are not as effective. There may also be additives which counteract any goodness in the fruits and vegetables. Unless you are present when juices are prepared, you cannot be 100 percent sure of their ingredients.

Rapid assimilation

Not only do pure juiced fruits and vegetables make a delicious addition to your diet, but the nutrients they contain are utilized by the body far more quickly than those the body gets from solid food, which requires many hours of digestion before any nourishment is available to the cells and tissues. At first you may find that due to the diuretic effect of the fruit and vegetable juices you are drinking, you are passing water more often than usual, and that you have a slight headache. Once your body gets used to the detoxifying effects of the juices these symptoms will fade.

All round good health

If you suffer from certain ailments, or are determined to prevent diseases such as heart disease, there are some combinations of fruits and vegetables that can help. Pioneers of nutritional therapy such as N. W. Walker and Max Gerson have long advocated the use of juices as part of a remedial treatment plan for many degenerative conditions. But, remember, while juicing is no doubt beneficial to your overall health, it should only be used to complement your daily eating plan. It is still necessary to ensure that you are eating enough from the other food groups to make sure that your body maintains strong bones and healthy cells.

If you are following a specially prescribed diet, or are under medical supervision, it is always recommended that you discuss any drastic changes with your health practitioner before beginning any new health regime.

juicing for
optimum health

The main benefits of juicing are, of course, the vitamins and minerals present in the fruit and vegetables. Vital nutrients such as folic acid, antioxidants, vitamins A, B, C and E, calcium, potassium, zinc, and amino acids are present in fresh fruit and vegetables, and are all necessary to ensure optimum health. Juicing is a natural, easy way to ensure that your daily intake of necessary vitamins is met.

Another important nutrient group present in juices is enzymes, which are responsible for the digestion and absorption of food into your body. Enzymes also convert foods into body tissue and are an important producer of energy levels. Without enzymes, our metabolism cannot function at its maximum rate. Fresh juice is the best way for your body to receive sources of enzymes. This is primarily because cooking vegetables destroys enzymes, which cannot exist in temperatures higher than 237°F. To enjoy the benefits that enzymes bring, it is best to eat as much raw produce as possible.

Protection against disease
A diet that is high in fruits and vegetables can prevent and help to cure a wide range of ailments. Plant chemicals, known as phytochemicals, hold the key to preventing deadly diseases, such as cancer and heart disease, as well as some of our most common, such as asthma and arthritis.

The phytochemicals that researchers have uncovered are changing the way we think about food, especially fruits and vegetables.

For example, broccoli and other cruciferous vegetables contain compounds such as dithiolthiones, which speed up the action of the enzymes involved in the body's detoxification process. This produces a flood of molecules called glutathiones, which can destroy toxins such as carcinogens. A regular intake of these vegetables is necessary for cancer prevention. Citrus fruits contain other compounds which help the body rid itself of carcinogens. They are also rich in pectin, which helps lower blood cholesterol levels, but in order to benefit from this the pith and cellular membranes of the fruit must also be juiced. Grapes contain a phytochemical that seems to protect each cell's DNA from damage. Similarly, a number of green vegetables contain phytochemicals that appear to offer protection against cancer-causing agents. The list goes on and on: bok choy, broccoli, cabbage, cauliflower, carrots, kale, peppers, garlic, onions, leeks and chives are but a few of the vegetables that appear to contain cancer-preventing phytochemicals. The problem, though, is that most of us don't eat enough fruits and vegetables to reap the benefits they offer. For example, although the American National Cancer Institute recommends eating five servings of vegetables and three of fruits each day, the average American eats only 1½ servings of vegetables and, on average, no fruit on any given day. British eating habits are not much better, with 65 percent of adults eating only one serving of fruit and vegetables per day.

Traditional nutrients

Fruit and vegetable juices are also good sources of traditional nutrients. Citrus fruits provide vitamin C. Carrot juice contains vitamin A, in the form of beta-carotene. A number of green juices are a good source of vitamin E. Fruit juices provide essential minerals such as iron, copper, potassium, sodium, and iodine, which are bound by the plant in a form that is most easily assimilated during digestion. As juicing removes the indigestible fiber, these nutrients are available to the body in much larger quantities than if the piece of fruit or vegetable were eaten whole. For example, when you eat a raw carrot you are only able to assimilate about 1 percent of the available beta-carotene, because many of the nutrients are trapped in the fiber. When a carrot is juiced, removing the fiber, nearly 100 percent of the beta-carotene can be assimilated. Finally, fruits and vegetables provide water. More than 65 percent of the cells in the human body are made up of water, and in some tissues the cells can be as much as 80 percent water. Water is essential for good health, yet most people don't consume enough. Many of the fluids we do drink—tea, coffee, alcohol and artificially flavored drinks —contain substances that require extra water for the body to eliminate, and tend to be dehydrating. Fruit and vegetable juices are free of these unnecessary substances.

What does juicing protect me from?

Besides providing your body with the vitamins and nutrients needed for good health, the antioxidants present in fruit and vegetables are nature's secret weapon against aging. So what causes aging? It is now accepted that free-radical damage contributes greatly to the aging process. Free radicals are highly reactive molecules that lack an electron. They attack cells to steal an electron to make them stable, and damage the cells in the process. The damaged cells then become free radicals. Free-radical damage contributes to wrinkles, loss of muscle tone and the onset of age-related diseases, and we need antioxidants to combat them.

We might not be aware that we are consuming antioxidants when we drink a glass of juice, but we will have achieved our daily intake if we juice four or five fruits and vegetables. We are also much more likely to continue with healthy meals throughout the rest of the day if we have begun the day in the right way.

how to juice

The first step in juicing is deciding which type of juicer to buy. They range from basic juice machines to more expensive hi-tech ones. Juicers work by separating the juice from the pulp, and although it is possible to juice by hand, this tends to be a time-consuming and messy process. Visit a department store and examine each machine thoroughly. Look for a juicer with a reputable brand name, with an opening big enough to fit larger fruits and vegetables, and make sure it is easy to take apart and clean. There are several types of juicers, so make sure you buy the best machine for your needs.

Citrus juicer
If you're keen to begin juicing, then it's likely that you've already got one of the simplest

pieces of equipment in your kitchen. The citrus juicer, or lemon squeezer, is ideal for extracting the juice from oranges, lemons, limes and grapefruit. This form of juicing is perfect if you just want to add a small amount of citrus juice to another liquid. Pure citrus juice has a high acid content, which may upset or irritate your stomach. If you want to enjoy pure citrus juice, dilute it with some water and enjoy the fruits of your labors!

Centrifugal juicer
The centrifugal juicer is the most widely used and affordable juicer available on the market. It works by centrifugal force, which means that when fresh fruits and vegetables are fed into a rapidly spinning grater, it separates the pulp from the juice. The pulp is retained in the machine while the juice runs into a separate pitcher, ready for tasting. If you're a true juicing aficionado, it is important to realize that a centrifugal juicer produces a smaller amount of juice than a masticating juicer, and some nutritionists believe this means that fewer nutrients are gained.

Masticating juicer
A more expensive version of the juicer, this machine works by pulverizing the fruit and vegetables and pushing them through a wire mesh with immense force. This process extracts a large amount of juice and therefore nutrients. As mentioned previously, juicing fresh produce is much better for you than heating or cooking foods, as a large proportion of the enzymes in the vegetables

are lost in cooking. As the masticating juicer doesn't use blades, this process avoids overheating and destroying some of the goodness in the ingredients.

Hydraulic press

If you visit a juice bar, you'll see that they use an expensive, shiny machine, which can juice and pulp large quantities. Unless you're intending to set up your own juice bar, it's quite unlikely that you'll need one of these machines.

Cleaning the juicer

The only downside to juicing is cleaning the juicer. The pulp and juice can make a mess, and the juicer will need thorough cleaning each time you use it. Look for a machine that dismantles easily, otherwise cleaning it becomes an annoying task and you may be discouraged from using it. When you are cleaning your machine, make sure you do a thorough job, as any residue left may harbor bacterial growth. (Many juicers come with a small brush, but a toothbrush or nailbrush work equally well for removing stubborn residual pulp.) You can leave the equipment to soak in warm soapy water, which will loosen the residue from those hard-to-reach places. A solution of one part white vinegar to two parts water will lessen any staining from the fruits and vegetables.

13

preparing produce

As most enzymes, vitamins and minerals lie just below the surface of fruit and vegetable skins, keep the skins on and wash all fruit and vegetables thoroughly in warm water. Some nutritionists suggest washing non-organic produce with a little dish-washing liquid and warm water, then rinsing it with cold water.

Preparing ingredients for the juicer

Foods must be cut into manageable pieces before juicing. Tear any vegetables that are soft enough, as this will also help to retain more nutrients. It's best to prepare your ingredients just before using them so that fewer nutrients are lost through oxidization. Some people are unsure whether to include seeds, pits, skin and outer leaves in their juices. The answer is that if the ingredients are not organic, do not include stems, skins or roots, but if the produce is organic, you can put everything in the juicer. However, don't include the skins from pineapple, mango, papaya, orange, lemon and banana, and remove the pits from apricots, peaches, mangoes and plums. You can include melon seeds, particularly watermelon, as these are full of juice. If you're making grape juice, choose green grapes with an amber tinge, or black grapes with a darkish bloom. Leave the pith on lemons.

Buying your ingredients

Steer clear of older fruit and vegetables, though, as the amount of goodness you extract is directly related to the freshness of the ingredients. Choose produce which is truest in color. After all, one of the reasons for juicing is to be positive that you have personally selected the ingredients. Packaged fruit juices do not carry such guarantees.

Frozen fruit and vegetables

Many supermarkets stock frozen produce, but is freezing a good thing? Yes, according to nutritionists, as long as it is done immediately after picking. Nothing beats fresh produce, but if there is nothing else available, the fruit stored in your freezer will provide a decent amount of the nutrients and vitamins necessary for your daily intake.

Buy organic

Following the recent GM debate, it was found that fruits and vegetables contained pesticides caused by spraying. Devotees of organic food enthuse over its extra taste and juiciness, and research has shown that levels of zinc, vitamin C and carotene are higher in organic produce. This is one of the benefits of buying organic—you gain more nutrients.

SUPPLEMENTS

Are supplements, tinctures and powders really necessary if you are already receiving your daily intake of nutrients? Some, such as spirulina, wheatgrass and aloe vera, are concentrated sources of the vitamins and minerals essential to good health and speedy recovery.

Spirulina is a form of chlorophyll, from the blue-green algae family. It is high in phosphorus, potassium, sodium, vitamin B3 and beta-carotene, and is available as a blue-green or white powder. Devotees of this alga enthuse about its energizing properties, and its main benefits are cell regeneration and renewal, good for halting the signs of aging; it is also antifungal and antibacterial. Spirulina is good for juices. It is not an ideal powder to take in water, and it's better to disguise the taste in your favorite juice. However, your pretty colored drinks will turn sludgy green.

Wheatgrass is not to everyone's taste, but including it in a juice is an easy way to receive its benefits. Rich in chlorophyll, wheatgrass is grown from wheat berries and is an ideal energizer and immunity booster.

Aloe Vera has immense immunity-boosting, antiviral and antiseptic properties, and it is particularly recommended for joint problems and irritable bowel syndrome—IBS. It has a very bitter taste, so mixed in a juice is an ideal way to take it.

Adding and subtracting

You can also add extra ingredients such as nuts, seeds or tinctures to your daily juices. Pumpkin seeds, for example, are full of folic acid and essential fatty oils, which are vital for healthy skin and nails. Many fruit juices have a high sugar content so, for daily juicing, many nutritionists recommend diluting them with mineral water. If citrus juices prove too tart and acidic, include a bland ingredient such as banana.

Storing your juice

The nutritional value of fruit and vegetable juices tends to deteriorate with storage as many vitamins oxidize on exposure to air. In order to obtain the maximum nutritional benefit, it is best to drink your juices as soon as you have made them. Fruits and vegetables (except bananas and avocados) will keep well in the refrigerator or a cool larder, but organic produce tends to spoil quickly—a sure sign of its freshness.

the best ingredients for juicing

Apple

Rich in: Beta-carotene, folic acid, vitamin C, calcium, magnesium, phosphorus, potassium, pectin. Also: Copper, zinc and vitamins B1, B2, B3, B6 and E. **Health benefits:** A delicious, sweet juice that is a good base. An ideal antioxidant, good for cleansing and the digestive system. Immune system booster.

Apricot

Rich in: Beta-carotene, vitamin C, papain, calcium, magnesium, phosphorus, potassium, flavonoids. Also: B vitamins, iron, zinc. **Health benefits:** Excellent antioxidant, cleanser and immune system booster. Apricots do not have much juice, so must be mixed with another juice or diluted with water or lemon juice.

Artichoke (globe)

Rich in: Magnesium, phosphorus, potassium, sodium, folic acid, beta-carotene, vitamin B3, vitamin C, vitamin K. **Health benefits:** Excellent for cleansing the liver, diuretic, lowers cholesterol.

Avocado

Rich in: Vitamin E, potassium, monounsaturated fat, vitamin B. **Health benefits:** Avocados are ideal for the skin and healing wounds as well as satisfying hunger. As they are high in vitamin E, they are also good for people who have cardiovascular disease. Vitamin E is also an immune booster.

Banana

Rich in: Beta-carotene, vitamin C, folic acid, magnesium, calcium, phosphorus, potassium. Also: Iron, B vitamins, zinc. **Health benefits:** Banana is a tasty juice to mix with berries and other ingredients. Ideal as an energy booster and for meals on the run.

Beets

Rich in: Folate, folic acid, soluble fibre. **Health benefits:** As well as being low in calories, beets are an ideal juice for pregnant women, as it provides high levels of folate, which can reduce the risk of spina bifida in unborn children.

Blackberry

Rich in: Beta-carotene, vitamins C and E, calcium, magnesium, phosphorus, potassium, sodium. **Health benefits:** A powerful antioxidant and ideal mixing juice, great for the immune system and has anti-aging properties.

Blackcurrant

Rich in: Beta-carotene, vitamins C and E, calcium, magnesium, phosphorus, potassium. Also: B vitamins, copper, iron. **Health benefits:** Ideal mixer with apple

as its taste is strong. A powerful antioxidant, anti-inflammatory and an immune system booster.

Broccoli
Rich in: Beta-carotene, folate, vitamin C, potassium, iron.
Health benefits: Rich in phytonutrients, which help to fight cancers.

Brussels sprouts
Rich in: Potassium, beta-carotene, folate, vitamin C.
Health benefits: Highest producer of folate, necessary for the production of white cells.

Cabbage
Rich in: Vitamin C, folate, beta-carotene and fiber. **Health benefits:** May help prevent and treat breast cancer, stomach ulcers, mastitis and heart disease.

Carrot
Rich in: Beta-carotene and alpha-carotene. **Health benefits:** Good mixer and energy food, and useful for the stomach and digestive system. Has diuretic properties and is used as a treatment for heartburn. Studies have shown carrots may protect against cancers of the mouth and rectum.

Celery
Rich in: Phytonutrients and apiin.

Health benefits: Excellent for cleansing the digestive system of uric acid. Used by sufferers from gout and urinary infections. Can help reduce inflammation in arthritis sufferers.

Cherry
Rich in: Beta-carotene, vitamin C, folic acid, calcium, magnesium, phosphorus, potassium, flavonoids. **Health benefits:** As there isn't much juice in cherries, the juice is best diluted. Cherries are great for boosting the immune system, as they contain a powerful antioxidant.

Chicory
Rich in: Potassium, beta-carotene, folate. **Health benefits:** Ideal for maintaining a healthy colon, reducing stress levels, anemia and preventing osteoporosis.

Chive
Rich in: Plant chemicals. **Health benefits:** Stimulates appetite.

Cinnamon
Rich in: We don't eat a large enough amounts of spices to receive nutrients from them. **Health benefits:** Relieves symptoms of colds, stomach chills, arthritis and poor circulation. Good for relieving indigestion and diarrhea.

17

Coriander (ground)

Rich in: We don't eat a large enough quantity of spices to receive nutrients from them. **Health benefits:** Can reduce inflammation, reduces symptoms of the menopause.

Cranberry

Rich in: Vitamin C, potassium, carotenes, fiber. **Health benefits:** Excellent for urinary tract infections as it stops *E. coli* bacteria from attaching to the walls of the urinary tract.

Cucumber

Rich in: Potassium, beta-carotene, silicon, sulphur, sodium, phosphorus. **Health benefits:** Probably the best diuretic known, great for hair growth, flushing out excess uric acid, and for skin nutrients.

Dandelion

Rich in: Iron, copper. **Health benefits:** Good for people suffering from fluid retention and high blood pressure.

Fennel

Rich in: Vitamin C. **Health benefits:** Diuretic effect, good for detoxifying the system.

Garlic

Rich in: Potassium, calcium, magnesium. **Health benefits:** Antiviral properties, good for fighting colds and infections.

Ginger

Rich in: Zinc, selenium. **Health benefits:** Helps to relieve coughs and colds.

Grape

Rich in: Glucose, fructose, potassium, vitamin C, carotenes. **Health benefits:** Fights carcinogens, relieves symptoms of arthritis, lowers blood pressure and helps urinary disorders. Contains the phytonutrient ellagic acid, which may deplete cancer-causing substances in the body.

Grapefruit

Rich in: Vitamin C, potassium, calcium, carotenes, folate. **Health benefits:** Good for protecting eyes from cataracts, aiding digestion and helping recovery from hangovers. Also recommended for protection against colon and stomach cancers.

Horseradish

Rich in: Potassium, calcium, folate, vitamin C. **Health benefits:** Excellent diuretic and good for digestion. Good for soothing respiratory problems.

Jerusalem artichoke

Rich in: Potassium, niacin, inutase, inulin. **Health benefits:** Because the inulin is converted into levulose by the enzyme inutase, diabetics can eat these.

Kale

Rich in: Beta-carotene, folate, calcium, potassium. **Health benefits:** The high levels of beta-carotene help to keep eyes strong and healthy. Good for stimulating the immune system.

Lemon

Rich in: Vitamin C, potassium, calcium, fructose. **Health benefits:** A good diuretic, with natural antibiotic properties which are good for treating colds, flu and coughs.

Lettuce

Rich in: Beta-carotene, folate, potassium. **Health benefits:** May help body to protect against cancer. Good food for pregnant women to help protect against spina bifida. Also recommended for keeping the colon healthy.

Lime

Rich in: Vitamin C, potassium, carotenes and calcium. **Health benefits:** Useful for treating infection from parasites. Cleanses and improves blood circulation and the nervous system.

Live natural yogurt

Rich in: Calcium, vitamin D. **Health benefits:** Helps to maintain good health, as it contains cultures with health-giving properties.

Mango

Rich in: Vitamin C, carotenes, fiber and B vitamins. **Health benefits:** Controls blood pressure, alleviates anemia, immune booster to fight infections.

Melon

Rich in: Calcium, magnesium, potassium, phosphorus, vitamin C, beta-carotene. **Health benefits:** Cleanser and rehydrator.

Mint

Rich in: Calcium, iron, magnesium, folate. **Health benefits:** Freshens breath, aids digestion, rejuvenator.

Onion

Rich in: Antioxidants, potassium, calcium. **Health benefits:** Useful for fighting colds, increases circulation.

Orange

Rich in: Vitamin C, potassium, carotenes, lutein. **Health benefits:** An ideal way to achieve your RDA of vitamin C, as well as good for fighting colds, lowering cholesterol and providing anti-cancer properties.

19

Papaya

Rich in: Vitamin C, antioxidants, potassium. **Health benefits:** Contains the enzyme papain, which helps to break down protein. As well as protecting your body against cancer, papaya is also an ideal fruit for smokers as it replaces the lost levels of vitamin C.

Parsley

Rich in: Vitamin C. **Health benefits:** Excellent breath freshener, maintains the skin's collagen structure.

Parsnip

Rich in: Niacin, B vitamins, folate and vitamin C. **Health benefits:** Good for diuretic properties and cleansing the liver and gallbladder.

Peach

Rich in: Antioxidant carotenes, flavonoids and vitamin C. **Health benefits:** Ideal for irritated stomachs, persistent coughs, reducing high blood pressure, as well as protecting against cancer and heart disease.

Pear

Rich in: Potassium, beta-carotene, vitamin C. **Health benefits:** Good for people with diabetes, and those watching their weight, as pears cause a slow but steady rise in blood sugar levels. If you are weaning a child, pears are ideal, as they rarely cause allergic reactions.

Pineapple

Rich in: Antioxidant vitamin C, bromelain, potassium, beta-carotene. **Health benefits:** Bromelain, the enzyme present in pineapple, has been shown to be effective in treating blood clots which may lead to thrombosis. Also aids digestion.

Potato

Rich in: Potassium, fiber, folate, vitamin C, carotenes and calcium. **Health benefits:** Good for treating lung cancer, preventing blood clots and reducing risk of heart disease.

Prune

Rich in: Fiber, potassium, iron, calcium, beta-carotene. **Health benefits:** Ideal for detoxifying and treating constipation, prune juice is best drunk at room temperature first thing in the morning. Prunes are also ideal for vegetarians as they are high in iron.

Radish

Rich in: Calcium, potassium, folate. **Health benefits:** Helps relieve mucus, helps prevent blood clotting, decreases risk of lung and stomach cancer.

Raspberry

Rich in: Phytonutrient ellagic acid, magnesium, potassium, vitamin C. **Health benefits:** Regulating menstrual cycles, fighting viral disease, and weight loss.

Soy

Rich in: Calcium and protein.
Health benefits: As an alternative to dairy products, soy is good for people who are lactose-intolerant or vegan but still require calcium to ward off osteoporosis.

Spinach

Rich in: Iron, folate, beta-carotene, calcium. **Health benefits:** One of the most highly recommended foods for women, particularly vegetarians, as it is a useful tool for protection against osteoporosis. It is also useful in detoxifying the body.

Strawberry

Rich in: Vitamin C, potassium, calcium, magnesium, phosphorus. **Health benefits:** A great antioxidant juice, with a marvelous taste and energizing properties.

Sweet potato

Rich in: Vitamin C, vitamin E, beta-carotene. **Health benefits:** Ideal for protecting against cancers.

Tomato

Rich in: Vitamin C, fiber, lycopene, beta-carotene, potassium, folate. **Health benefits:** An ideal juice for lowering the risk of cancer and heart disease, due to the presence of the antioxidant lycopene. Lycopene is also responsible for protecting joints, muscles and brain cells.

Turnip

Rich in: Iron, beta-carotene, vitamin B, vitamin C. **Health benefits:** Ideal food for people watching their weight, as turnips are high in carbohydrates but low in fat.

Watercress

Rich in: Iron, vitamin C, beta-carotene. **Health benefits:** Good for treating lung cancer, muscle cramps and night blindness.

Watermelon

Rich in: Beta-carotene, folic acid, vitamin B5, vitamin C, calcium, magnesium, phosphorus, potassium. **Health benefits:** Yields a large amount of juice. A great antioxidant, detoxing and diuretic fruit.

Yam

Rich in: Potassium, calcium, folate, fiber. **Health benefits:** The Mexican wild yam is a natural contraceptive, and also relaxes muscles so is good for PMT and soothing the stomach.

Meal plans

Detox

After years of irregular meals, fast and processed foods and toxins, your body will respond quickly to detoxification, which will leave you feeling energized and with an overall sense of well-being. As detoxifying will result in an initial loss of excess fluids, this is an ideal way to start your new eating plan. Diets don't work. The only way to ensure a healthy weight loss and begin a sensible eating plan is a detox. Don't attempt a lengthy detoxification program though. You may begin it with the best of intentions, but break it on the third day out of sheer hunger. Try a weekend-long detox plan, or even a one-day plan, and concentrate on the juices that speed the detoxification process and aid digestion and the immune system.

A one-day juice detox is beneficial for two reasons. First, you'll be clearing your body of a build-up of toxins, which could be contributing to certain ailments. Second, although you may feel slightly tired or headachy as your body goes without sugars or caffeine, it is still a day dedicated solely to you, to relax and rejuvenate. Don't arrange appointments, and, if you want to exercise, don't do anything strenuous. Whatever you do do, make sure it's something you enjoy. There are no hard and fast rules for a one-day detox, as long as you spend the entire day looking after yourself.

Your questions answered
When should I detox?

If you've been over-indulging and are feeling lethargic, listless and bloated.

How long should I detox?

Don't detox for longer than a week, although you can repeat the process every few months. A one-day detox can be repeated every week.

Won't I just put the weight back on?

By eliminating the foods which are harmful, your body will feel lighter and less bloated (most people lose 2–3 pounds in the first week of detoxing). Continue the good work by keeping your intake of these foods moderate and replacing them with healthy alternatives.

Do not detox if you:
- Are underweight.
- Are pregnant or breast-feeding.
- Have anemia.
- Have Type 1 diabetes.
- Are taking any prescription medication.
- Have kidney failure.
- Have severe liver disease.

Four reasons to detox:
- Your skin becomes clearer.
- Your bowels become more regular.
- Liver and kidney function are more efficient.
- It reduces stress levels, hormone imbalances and other inflammatory conditions.

ONE-DAY DETOX

8.00 a.m.
Drink a glass of warm water with a little lemon juice. It's a gentle way to begin the day, and the combination will help to flush out the kidneys.

8.30 a.m.
Depending on how you're feeling, try a juice with a little citrus fruit in it, or apple, pineapple or melon (see Juicy Lucy, page 108 or Moody Blues, page 36). If this is the first time you've tried juicing, use a simple recipe such as carrot and apple, which will wake you up and begin the cleansing process.

9.00 a.m.
It's time to get your circulation moving! Dry skin brushing is ideal, as it stimulates the circulatory and lymphatic systems, as well as exfoliating any dead cells which can make your skin look dull. Using a natural bristle brush, begin at your feet, and with long, smooth movements gently move upward. When you've finished, hop in a warm shower and enjoy the feeling of running water on your tingling body. (You can finish with a blast of cold water if you're feeling brave!) After your shower, dry and moisturize your skin.

9.30 a.m.
Enjoy a glass of water or a herbal tea, such as peppermint, which will aid the detoxification process.

10.00 a.m.
If it's a nice day, go for a walk. By moving your body, you're less likely to feel the side-effects of a detox, such as

tiredness or headaches, and you'll also be helping your body rid itself of its toxins. If you don't fancy a walk, try yoga.

11.30 a.m.
When you've finished exercising, have another glass of water or herbal tea.

12.30 p.m.
It's lunchtime, so you need a filling juice to alleviate hunger pains and reduce the temptation to snack. Try a combination of root vegetables and greens, e.g. cucumber, spinach and beets (see Magnificent 7, page 107).

1 p.m.
Have another glass of water, or a cup of herbal tea if you prefer. Try ginger, which is good for the stomach, or lemon, another good tea for detoxification.

1.30 p.m.
A detox program can be quite tiring, as your body is ridding itself of a build-up of toxins which have taken years to accumulate. Either have a nap or lie down and read or listen to some relaxing music. Maybe do some stretching and breathing exercises. You'll probably lull yourself into a sleep anyway!

2.30 p.m.
Have another glass of water or herbal tea.

3.30 p.m.
Your blood sugar levels may be feeling a little low by now, so you can pack this juice full of fruits such as blueberries, strawberries, cranberries, oranges and mangoes (see

Sweet Chariot, page 116 or 'C' Breeze, page 104). It may taste slightly tart after a relatively food-free day, but you'll feel energized afterward.

5 p.m.
It's important to drink at least eight glasses of water every day, so have another glass now.

7.30 p.m.
Even though you'll probably have no problems going to sleep tonight, make sure you enjoy an evening juice which contains ingredients to aid relaxation and beat insomnia. Try juicing bananas, lettuce or apples (see Smooth Operator, page 61 or Sleep Tight, page 58).

9.30 p.m.
Have another glass of water and then your last herbal tea. So that you are ready for sleep, try a camomile tea, which has calming properties. Take a relaxing bath, adding some aromatherapy oils such as lavender, ylang ylang, rose and sandalwood. Make sure the bath water isn't too hot and, if you can, dim the lights and play some relaxing music.

10.00 p.m.
It's time for bed and you've completed your detox day. Remember that your stomach will be relatively empty by tomorrow morning, so don't celebrate your day with a fry-up, start off gradually with some fresh fruit and yogurt or whole-wheat toast and honey. Opt for a light salad lunch, and possibly some steamed vegetables and rice for dinner, supplemented of course by a couple of fresh nutritious juices.

RDA (Recommended Daily Allowance) chart

VITAMIN	FUNCTION	FOOD SOURCES
Vitamin A (retinol)	Promotes eye health; antioxidant with immunity-boosting function.	Liver, dairy products, eggs, oily fish.
Beta-carotene (pro-vitamin A)	Antioxidant, offers protection against cancer. The body can convert beta-carotene into vitamin A.	All dark green, orange or red fruit, e.g. red bell pepper, pumpkin and spinach.
Vitamin B1 (thiamine)	Needed for energy production, and for a healthy nervous system.	Milk, meat, whole-grain/fortified breakfast cereal, dried fruit, nuts, pulses, brown rice, peas and beans.
Vitamin B2 (riboflavin)	Helps the body to get energy from food. Aids healthy eyes, hair and nails.	Milk, liver, kidneys, cheese, fortified breakfast cereal.
Vitamin B5 (pantothenic acid)	Anti-stress vitamin, boosting the metabolism and aiding energy release from food.	Liver, kidneys, yeast, wheatgerm, fortified breakfast cereal, whole-wheat bread, nuts, pulses, fresh vegetables.
Vitamin B6 (pyridoxine)	Balances hormonal change in women and helps cell production.	Numerous foods, including meat, whole-wheat bread, brown rice, bananas and pulses.
Vitamin B12 (cobalamin)	Aids red blood cell production and maintenance of healthy nerves.	Liver, kidney, oily fish, meat, eggs, dairy products, fortified breakfast cereals.
Folic acid	Prevention of spinal disabilities in the fetus during pregnancy. Aids red blood cell production and the release of energy from food.	Green leafy vegetables, liver, pulses, eggs, wholemeal cereals, orange juice, wheatgerm.
Vitamin C (ascorbic acid)	Protects against some cancers and coronary heart disease. Helps healthy bones, teeth and gums.	Most fruit and vegetables—among the best sources are kiwi fruits, citrus fruits, peppers, blackcurrants and strawberries.
Vitamin D (calciferol)	Promotes a healthy nervous system; formation of healthy bones and teeth.	Oily fish, dairy products, eggs.
Vitamin E (tocopherols)	Antioxidant, protecting cells from free-radical damage. Protects against heart disease and cancer.	Vegetable oils, polyunsaturated margarine, wheatgerm, sunflower seeds, hazelnuts, oily fish, whole-grain cereal, eggs, avocado and spinach.
Vitamin K	Necessary in the formation of blood clots when the body needs it.	Broccoli, cabbage, spinach, liver, alfafa, tomatoes and kelp.

DAILY DOSAGE	VITAL INFORMATION
600 mcg	High vitamin A intake is unsafe during pregnancy (although beta-carotene is fine).
25 mg	A high intake of beta-carotene from supplements can turn the skin yellow.
0.8 mg	Vitamin B1 is easily lost into cooking water. To counteract this, use this water for gravies and sauces.
1.3 mg	Overdoses of Vitamin B2 can lead to a loss of other B vitamins through urine.
No official RDA	Vitamin B5 deficiency is exceptionally rare and has not been thoroughly studied.
1.2 mg	The pill, antibiotics and smoking all increase the need for vitamin B6. Supplements can help relieve PMT symptoms.
1.5 mg	Vitamin B12 is only in foods of animal origin, so vegetarians and vegans need supplements.
200 mg	All women of child-bearing age should take a folic acid supplement. The need is increased if you are taking the pill.
40 mg	Vitamin C is damaged by storage and cooking. Cook vegetables for as short a time as possible and serve immediately. If you have had kidney stones, check with a doctor before taking supplements.
10 mg	If you aren't getting any sun, or are pregnant or breastfeeding, then take a supplement. Check with your doctor first if you have sarcoidosis.
10 mg	The pill increases vitamin E demand. The vitamin E contained in vegetable oils is killed by high temperatures (including deep-frying).
10 mg	Only take K supplements under your doctor's advice if you're taking anti-coagulant medication.

Ailment chart

Anemia	Iron Maiden, Kale and Hearty
Arthritis	Twister, Magnificent 7
Asthma	Root 66, Magnificent 7, Heart Beet, Loosen Up 1, Loosen Up 2
Bloating/Water Retention	Six Pack, Flush-a-bye-baby, Evergreen, Ginger Spice, Ginger Zinger
Bronchitis	Chili Queen, Loosen Up 1, Loosen Up 2
Cellulite	Bumpy Ride, Energy Burst, Six Pack
Colds and Flu	Frisky Sour
Constipation	Way to Go, Magnificent 7, Easy Does It
Cholesterol Reduction	Purple Passion, Belly Berry
Cystitis	Flush-a-bye-baby, "C" Breeze
Detox	Juicy Lucy, Flush-a-bye-baby, Spring Clean, Red Rocket
Diarrhea	Belly Berry, Purple Passion
Diabetes	Famous 5
Dieting	Ginger Spice, Evergreen, Green Peace, Six Pack, Kale and Hearty
Eyesight	Vision Impeccable, Twister
Good for Children	Bugsy Banana, Super Shakey, Strawberry Sunrise, Tummy Tickler, Maybe Baby
Hemorrhoids	Easy Does It, Way to Go
Hair and Nails	Hard as Nails, Earth Mother
Hangover	Morning After
Headaches and Migraines	Head Banger, Evergreen
Heart Disease	Heart Beet, Root 66, Bumpy Ride
High Blood Pressure	Lounge Lizard, Hard as Nails
Hypoglycemia	Energy Burst, Magnificent 7

Immune System	Ginger Zinger, Chili Queen, "C" Breeze, Frisky Sour, Morning After
Insomnia	Sleep Tight, Evergreen, Smooth Operator
Irritable Bowel Syndrome	Red Rocket, Spring Clean
Lethargy	Power Pack, Juicy Lucy
Low Energy	Kale and Hearty
Low Fertility	Passion Thriller, Green Dream, Cool Down, Heart Beet, Earth Mother
Meals in a Minute	Green Dream, Magnificent 7, Passion Thriller
Menopause	Cool Down, Root 66
Morning Sickness	Peach Fizz, Quantum Leap
Motion Sickness	Quantum Leap, Peach Fizz
Osteoporosis	Sticks and Stones, Root 66
PMT	Moody Blues, Sleep Tight
Pregnancy Care	Earth Mother, Cool Down
Seasonal Affective Disorder	Smooth Operator, Bugsy Banana
Sinusitis	Loosen Up 1, Loosen Up 2, Chilli Queen
Skin Disorders	Herbi-four, Magnificent 7, Red Rocket
Skin Eruptions	Hot Potato, Cool Down
Stomach Ulcer	Well Healed, Red Rocket
Stress	Evergreen, Lounge Lizard
Weight Gain	Sweet Chariot, Bugsy Banana, Green Dream, Passion Thriller

the juices

Cystitis. Sometimes known as the "honeymoon disease," cystitis is a painful urinary infection which causes a burning sensation when passing urine. The symptoms can be relieved by drinking as much liquid as possible, particularly juices containing cranberries. SEE ALSO "c" breeze

flush-a -bye-baby

The cucumber in this juice provides protective antioxidants for the digestive tract and, combined with the melon, acts as a diuretic to cleanse the intestinal system. **Makes about ¾ cup**

8 oz cranberries
8 oz watermelon or
galia melon
8 oz cucumber

Juice all the ingredients, including the seeds of the melon and the skin of the cucumber. Serve in a tumbler and decorate with melon sticks, if liked.

NUTRITIONAL VALUES
vitamin A 8,475 iu
vitamin C 120 mg
potassium 880 mg
iron 4.7 mg
calcium 92.5 mg
232 calories

Thrush. *Candida albicans* is a common yeast which lives harmlessly in all of us. However, in some cases of low immunity, it can travel through the vaginal tract and cause thrush. Symptoms include mood swings and depression, recurrent vaginal yeast and chronic digestive problems. Cut out junk food, fats, sugar and highly processed foods to discourage the growth of yeast.

culture shock

All the ingredients in this juice have antibacterial properties. It is particularly effective if you are taking antibiotics. **Makes about ¾ cup**

8 oz apple
3½ oz frozen cranberries
3½ oz live natural yogurt
1 tablespoon clear honey

Juice the apple and whizz in a blender with the other ingredients. Serve in a tumbler over ice cubes.

NUTRITIONAL VALUES
vitamin C 20 mg
calcium 40 mg
339 calories

Low fertility. With low sperm counts and lowered fertility levels, our reproductive abilities are one of the biggest causes of concern in today's society. Male fertility may be boosted by increasing intakes of vitamin E, zinc and iron. Women should look to increase their folic acid levels, as well as zinc and vitamin E.

SEE ALSO green dream, cool down, heart beet, earth mother

passion thriller

Avocado is rich in vitamin E, while apricots are an excellent source of zinc and iron. **Makes about ¾ cup**

**6 oz melon
(½ large melon)
4 oz cucumber
4 oz avocado
2 oz dried apricots
1 tablespoon wheatgerm**

Juice the melon and cucumber. Whizz in a blender with the avocado, apricots, wheatgerm and a couple of ice cubes. Decorate with dried apricot slivers, if liked.

NUTRITIONAL VALUES
vitamin A 8,738 iu
vitamin C 110 mg
vitamin E 2 mcg
potassium 1,470 mg
iron 1.6 mg
zinc 1.29 mg
357 calories

PMT. If you are one of the many women who suffer from monthly cramps, irritability and stomach upsets due to your menstrual cycle, then help is at hand! It is important to ensure that you are replacing your iron levels, as many women find that they are lethargic and tired during their period. If you also feel bloated due to water retention, or find that you gain weight just before your period, then certain fruits and vegetables may assist these symptoms. Your cycle may also affect your moods, so a calming juice may be just what you need to ensure that your cycle causes as little disruption as possible. SEE ALSO **sleep tight**

moody blues

Pineapples contain bromelain which is a great muscle relaxant, and blackberries are good sources of folic acid.

Makes about ¾ cup

12 oz blackberries
12 oz pineapple or
1 small pineapple

Juice the blackberries first, then the pineapple, to push through the pulp. Blend the juice with a couple of ice cubes and serve in a tall glass, decorated with a pineapple sliver, if liked.

NUTRITIONAL VALUES
vitamin A 658 iu
vitamin C 129.5 mg
iron 3.29 mg
potassium 1,081 mg
calcium 136 mg
folic acid 340 mcg
353 calories

37

GOOD FOR

Menopause. The menopause occurs when the amount of the hormones estrogen and progesterone produced by the ovaries decreases. This can be an extremely stressful time for women, as the menopause may cause irritability, hot flushes, mood swings, headaches, night sweats, vaginal dryness, loss of libido and anxiety. SEE ALSO root 66

cool down

Beets are a rich source of folate which can help to protect the heart, and, together with carrots, help to regulate hormones. Yam provides the hormone progesterone, which helps to replace the hormones lost when the menopause occurs. **Makes about ¾ cup**

6 oz carrot
3½ oz beets
6 oz yam or
    sweet potato
4 oz fennel

Juice all the ingredients. Mix well and serve in a glass with ice cubes. Decorate with fennel fronds, if liked.

NUTRITIONAL VALUES
vitamin A 49,430 iu
vitamin C 69.95 mg
iron 3.9 mg
folic acid 254 mcg
folate 196 mcg
296 calories

39

Bloating or water retention. This can be uncomfortable and painful. The problem can be caused by food allergies, hormonal imbalances, a lack of essential fatty acids in the diet, and also, ironically, by not drinking enough water. Zinc is essential to decrease water retention. SEE ALSO **flush-a-bye-baby, evergreen, ginger spice, ginger zinger**

six pack

All the ingredients in this juice contain high levels of zinc and potassium. This recipe is also great if you have just eaten a salty meal.

Makes about ¾ cup

4 oz asparagus stalks
10 dandelion leaves
4 oz melon
6 oz cucumber
7 oz pear

Trim the woody bits off the asparagus stalks. Roll the dandelion leaves into a ball and juice them (if you have picked wild leaves, wash them first) with the asparagus. Peel and juice the melon. Juice the cucumber and pear with their skins. Whizz everything in a blender and serve in a tall glass with ice cubes.

NUTRITIONAL VALUES
vitamin A 5,018 iu
vitamin C 87 mg
potassium 1,235 mg
zinc 1.36 mg
215 calories

Cellulite. The lumpy orange-peel skin that afflicts even the slimmest of women has baffled scientists and medical professionals for years. It is caused by the immobilization of fat cells, and if we eat a diet which is low in the saturated fats found in meat and dairy products, this will ensure that fat cells disperse. Large amounts of water to flush out toxins, as well as fruits and vegetables with a high water content, all help to eliminate cellulite. SEE ALSO **energy burst, six pack**

bumpy ride

Cleanses the whole system, blood, kidneys and lymph. The pectin in the apples strengthens the immune system.

Makes about ⅔ cup

7 oz apple
2 oz beets
3 oz celery

Juice together all the ingredients and serve over ice in a tumbler. Decorate with apple slices, if liked.

NUTRITIONAL VALUES
vitamin A 480 iu
vitamin C 23 mg
potassium 763 mg
magnesium 37 mg
179 calories

43

Asthma. The number of children afflicted with asthma has risen dramatically over the past few years, and pollutants, allergies and dust may all act as triggers. Juices, combined with certain breathing techniques and correct care, may help to lessen the severity of an attack. SEE ALSO **magnificent 7, heart beet, loosen up 1, loosen up 2**

root 66

The magnesium in the parsley has a calming effect; it is also present in celery. Garlic is renowned for its antibacterial, antibiotic, antiseptic and antiviral properties. **Makes about ¾ cup**

6 oz carrot
6 oz parsnip
6 oz celery
6 oz sweet potato
a handful of parsley
1 garlic clove

Juice all the ingredients together and whizz in a blender with 2 ice cubes. Serve in a wide glass decorated with a wedge of lemon and a parsley sprig, if liked.

NUTRITIONAL VALUES
vitamin A 51,192 iu
vitamin C 136.35 mg
potassium 2,882.5 mg
magnesium 150.5 mg
386 calories

GOOD FOR

Bronchitis. A persistent cough and the constant bringing up of mucus are two of the earliest symptoms of this chronic complaint, which causes constant wheezing and breathlessness. SEE ALSO **loosen up 1, loosen up 2**

chili queen

This juice is rich in vitamin C, which is great for fighting off bronchial illness. Enzymes in the pineapple dissolve mucus, and the chili is a great expectorant. Chilis are rich in carotenoids and vitamin C, and are thought to help increase blood flow; they also have antibacterial properties which make them a favorite for beating colds and flu.

Makes about ¾ cup

8 oz carrot
½ small deseeded chili or
 a sprinkling of chili
 powder
8 oz pineapple
½ lime
1 tablespoon chopped
 cilantro leaves

Juice the carrot, chili and pineapple. Serve in a tall glass over ice cubes. Squeeze in the lime juice and stir in the chopped cilantro leaves to serve.

NUTRITIONAL VALUES
vitamin A 70,382 iu
vitamin C 72 mg
selenium 3.95 mcg
zinc 0.73 mg
240 calories

47

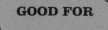
Colds and flu. If you're run down and haven't been eating a balanced diet, your immune system becomes more susceptible to colds and flu. At the first sign of symptoms, drinking juices with papaya, lemon, lime, garlic or ginger may help.

frisky sour

Papaya is an ideal juice for children, as it is more palatable than some other sweet juices. **Makes about ¾ cup**

5 oz papaya
5 oz grapefruit
5 oz raspberries
½ lime

Scoop out the flesh of the papaya, and juice it with the grapefruit (with the pith left on), and the raspberries. Squeeze in the lime juice and mix. Serve with a few ice cubes and, if liked, decorate with lime slices.

NUTRITIONAL VALUES
vitamin A 810 iu
vitamin C 188 mg
selenium 4.05 mcg
zinc 1.09 mg
193 calories

49

Sinusitis. Sinus problems occur when the nasal and sinus passages become inflamed. Keep away from smoky places and try to avoid exhaust fumes, dust and pollen. Dairy products and wheat are also mucus-forming, so cut these out of your diet, if you can, until your condition has improved. These two juices should be taken in tandem. SEE ALSO **chili queen**

loosen up 1

Horseradish stimulates capillary action and dissolves mucus in the nasal passages, while the vitamin C in lemon juice may help to lower a high temperature. **Makes about ¼ cup**

1½ teaspoons pulverized horseradish
½ lemon

Pulverize the horseradish by juicing a small amount and mixing the juice and the pulp. Put it into a shot glass and stir in the lemon juice. Take twice a day.

NUTRITIONAL VALUES
vitamin C 55 mg
selenium 0.4 mcg
zinc 0.18 mg
25 calories

loosen up 2

The radish juice is too strong to be taken alone, but combined with carrot it has the effect of soothing the membranes and cleansing the body of the mucus dissolved by the horseradish in Loosen Up 1. **Makes about ¾ cup**

6 oz carrot
3½ oz radishes, with tops and leaves
1 inch cube fresh ginger root, roughly chopped (optional)

Juice the carrot, radishes and ginger, if using. Add some ice cubes. Drink one hour after Loosen Up 1.

NUTRITIONAL VALUES
vitamin A 49,233 iu
vitmin C 40 mg
selenium 2.82 mcg
zinc 0.8 mg
115 calories

Stress. An unwelcome fact in the twenty-first century is that a large number of us are suffering from high levels of stress. Whether work-related, or due to personal problems, stress is now considered one of the major causes of illness today. High levels of stress deplete your body of essential nutrients, and can cause symptoms such as headaches, indigestion, irritability and joint pain. SEE ALSO **lounge lizard**

evergreen

This juice combines celery and fennel, which help the body utilize magnesium and calcium to calm the nerves. Coupled with the sedative effect of lettuce, it is an ideal stressbuster.

Makes about ¾ cup

2 oz celery
2 oz fennel
4 oz Romaine lettuce
6 oz pineapple
1 teaspoon chopped
tarragon

Juice all the ingredients and whizz in a blender with 2 ice cubes. Serve in a tall glass and decorate with tarragon sprigs, if liked.

NUTRITIONAL VALUES
vitamin A 3,437 iu
vitamin C 68 mg
magnesium 47 mg
calcium 95 mg
128 calories

53

Lethargy. Most people who juice regularly report an almost immediate increase in their energy levels. If you are feeling lethargic or constantly tired, try to avoid processed foods and cut out salt and refined sugars from your diet, as these tend to place a strain on your whole system. SEE ALSO juicy lucy

power pack

Carrots, beets and oranges are all high in vitamins A and C, antioxidants and phytonutrients such as alpha- and beta-carotene. This juice is also a rich source of potassium. A real tonic.

Makes about ¾ cup

8 oz carrot
4 oz beets
1 orange
4 oz strawberries

Juice the carrot, beets and orange. Put the juice into a blender with a couple of ice cubes and the strawberries. Whizz for 20 seconds and serve in a tall glass. Decorate with strips of orange rind, if liked.

NUTRITIONAL VALUES
vitamin A 70,652 iu
vitamin C 166 mg
potassium 1,646 mg
magnesium 91.5 mg
selenium 5.1 mcg
259 calories

SORTING OUT YOUR SYSTEM

Energy levels. This juice is a great energy booster with nutritional benefits that far outweigh its flavor.

kale and hearty

Spirulina is one the best sources of vitamin B12, which is essential for the functioning of all cells. Wheatgrass is high in chlorophyll, which combats anemia. Kale has as much usable calcium as milk. Need we say more?

Makes about ¼ cup

1 oz kale
3½ oz wheatgrass
1 teaspoon spirulina

Juice the kale and the wheatgrass; stir in the spirulina powder. Serve in a small glass decorated with wheatgrass blades.

NUTRITIONAL VALUES
vitamin A 7,740 iu
vitamin B12 8 mcg
vitamin C 91 mg
chlorophyll 643 mg
iron 52 mg
calcium 462 mg
30 calories

Insomnia. Sleeping tablets will offer only a short-term solution to insomnia and may actually exacerbate the problem. Alternative treatments are better for you in the long run. Be careful what you eat before bedtime, and follow a nightly, relaxing ritual. SEE ALSO **evergreen, smooth operator**

sleep tight

Pineapple and grapes give a boost of blood sugar, which can help to induce sleep. Lettuce and celery relax the nerves and muscles.

Makes about ¾ cup

4 oz pineapple (without skin)
4 oz grapes
2 oz lettuce
2 oz celery

Juice all the ingredients and serve in a tall glass over ice. Decorate with lettuce leaves, if liked.

NUTRITIONAL VALUES
vitamin C 50 mg
magnesium 35.2 mg
vitamin B6 0.3 mg
niacin 1.38 mg
tryptophan 4 mg
167 calories

Seasonal affective disorder. This is now recognized as a medical condition, affecting one in ten Britons every year. The symptoms include depression, insomnia, irritability, moodiness, lethargy, loss of appetite and weight gain during the winter months. SEE ALSO **bugsy banana**

smooth operator

Bananas and figs are rich in tryptophan which is necessary for production of serotonin, which can induce a feeling of well-being. Because these fruits are high in natural sugars, they produce a feeling of fullness which can help prevent overeating. **Makes about ¾ cup**

8 oz carrot
3½ oz figs
1 orange
1 inch cube fresh ginger root, roughly chopped
3½ oz banana

Juice the carrot, figs, orange and ginger. Put the juice into a blender with the banana and 2 ice cubes and whizz for 20 seconds for a delicious smoothie. Add more ice cubes and decorate with sliced figs, if liked.

NUTRITIONAL VALUES
vitamin A 14,117 iu
vitamin C 192 mg
magnesium 118 mg
vitamin B6 0.23 mg
tryptophan 89 mg
460 calories

Headaches and migraine. Juices are an ideal remedy for headaches and migraine as the nutritional benefits of the fruits and vegetables enter into your system quickly. SEE ALSO **evergreen**

head banger

Lettuce and fennel are extremely calming ingredients. They contain calcium and magnesium, which are antispasmodic and produce feelings of calm, that may alleviate head pain. **Makes about ¾ cup**

6 oz lettuce
4 oz fennel
½ lemon

Juice the lettuce, fennel and lemon, and serve on ice. Decorate with lemon slivers and lettuce leaves, if liked.

NUTRITIONAL VALUES
vitamin A 4,726 iu
vitamin C 67 mg
potassium 1,070 mg
calcium 124 mg
magnesium 32 mg
72 calories

63

GOOD FOR **Reducing cholesterol.** High cholesterol levels are caused by eating a diet containing too much saturated fat, which leads to a build-up along the inside walls of the arteries. SEE ALSO **belly berry**

purple passion

Grapefruit is particularly recommended for its rich source of vitamin C and bioflavonoids, which protect the health of the arteries. Blueberries are also extremely potent antioxidants and, along with apples, can help prevent hardening of the arteries and reduce cholesterol levels.

Makes about ¾ cup

8 oz blueberries
4 oz grapefruit
8 oz apple
1 inch cube fresh ginger root, roughly chopped

Juice all the ingredients and serve in a tall glass with ice cubes. Decorate with thin slices of ginger, if liked.

NUTRITIONAL VALUES
vitamin A 695 iu
vitamin C 134 mg
magnesium 59 mg
niacin 1.91 mg
vitamin B6 0.39 mg
vitamin E 3.12 mg
380 calories

High blood pressure. High blood pressure can be caused by blood clots and atherosclerosis (the formation of deposits in the arteries). Usually atherosclerosis also means that there is a hardening of the arteries, caused by a lack of vitamin C, which is needed to make collagen, the intercellular substance that keeps skin and arteries supple. SEE ALSO **hard as nails**

lounge lizard

The vitamin C and potassium-rich ingredients in this juice help to lower blood pressure. **Makes about ¾ cup**

8 oz kiwi fruit
4 oz cucumber
1 tablespoon
   pomegranate seeds
   (if available)

Wash the kiwi fruit and cucumber but do not peel them, as both contain nutrients in their skins. Juice both and serve with a slice of lime, if liked. If you wish, stir in a tablespoon of pomegranate seeds.

NUTRITIONAL VALUES
vitamin C 250 mg
potassium 1,010 mg
zinc 0.67 mg
168 calories

SORTING OUT YOUR SYSTEM

Hypoglycemia. Blood sugar levels drop when the muscles and liver break down glycogen stores into glucose, releasing it into the tissues. This may lead to fatigue, light-headedness and depression, so it is important to maintain your blood sugar levels in order to function consistently. Fruits contain high levels of natural sugar, so try to include vegetable juices in your eating plan. SEE ALSO **magnificent 7**

energy burst

This juice contains cinnamon, which is renowned for stabilizing blood sugar. To add an extra boost of glucose-regulating chromium, stir 1 tablespoon of raw wheatgerm into the finished juice.

Makes about ¾ cup

4 oz spinach
8 oz apple
3½ oz yellow bell pepper
a pinch of cinnamon

Juice all the ingredients and serve in a glass. If liked, add a cinnamon stick for decoration.

NUTRITIONAL VALUES
vitamin C 175 mg
magnesium 235 mg
potassium 2,125 mg
zinc 1.54 mg
222 calories

Diabetes. Unquenchable thirst and passing abnormal amounts of urine are among the first signs of diabetes. The disorder occurs when the pancreas fails to produce enough insulin—the hormone that regulates the blood sugar level. (Warning: since diabetes is a serious illness, medical advice is imperative, especially if the sufferer is a child.)

famous 5

This juice contains the top five vegetables that produce natural insulin.

Makes about ¾ cup

3½ oz Brussels sprouts
3½ oz carrot
3½ oz Jerusalem
  artichokes
3½ oz green beans
3½ oz lettuce
½ lemon

Wash all the vegetables and juice them with the lemon. Serve decorated with slivers of green bean and carrot, if liked.

NUTRITIONAL VALUES
vitamin A 31,642 iu
vitamin C 145 mg
zinc 1 mg
186 calories

SORTING OUT YOUR SYSTEM

Anemia. If you lack iron in your diet (possibly due to a vegetarian diet, or a heavy menstrual cycle) then you may have anemia, which can leave you feeling lethargic, depressed, or prone to flu and colds. SEE ALSO **kale and hearty**

iron maiden

Folic acid builds up red blood cells, chlorophyll helps to combat fatigue, and spirulina provides a valuable boost of vitamin B12.

Makes about ¾ cup

8 oz spinach
1 oz parsley
8 oz carrot
1 teaspoon spirulina

Juice the spinach, parsley and carrot, and stir in the spirulina. Serve in a tumbler, decorated with carrot slivers if liked.

NUTRITIONAL VALUES
vitamin C 450 mg
folic acid 235 mg
chlorophyll 100 mg
vitamin B12 20 mcg
229 calories

Hemorrhoids. The medical name for piles, hemorrhoids are caused by swollen veins inside or outside of the anus. They can cause itching and pain, and are the most common source of anal bleeding. Sometimes a blood clot or a thrombus turns a pile into a hard, extremely painful lump. SEE ALSO **way to go**

easy does it

The watercress helps to dissolve the coagulated blood fibrin, and the pear helps to regulate bowel movement. **Makes about ¼ cup**

8 oz pear
4 oz watercress
½ lemon

Juice the ingredients and serve over ice. Add a twist of lemon, if liked.

NUTRITIONAL VALUES
vitamin A 5,935 iu
vitamin C 85 mg
calcium 185 mg
vitamin B6 0.2 mg
172 calories

Heart disease. This is one of the most preventable diseases in today's society. An increased intake of fried and fatty foods, a high salt intake, stress, smoking and lack of exercise are all contributory factors. Boosting your intake of vitamin C and vitamin E and taking regular exercise can add as many as ten years to your life.

SEE ALSO **root 66, bumpy ride**

heart beet

The onion and garlic thin the blood and help to lower cholesterol. Watercress oxygenates the blood and beets build up the red blood cells.

Makes about ¾ cup

4 oz beets
4 oz watercress
4 oz red onion
8 oz carrot
1 garlic clove

Juice the ingredients and serve in a tall glass. Decorate with beet leaves and watercress, if liked.

NUTRITIONAL VALUES
vitamin A 41,166 iu
vitamin C 85 mg
magnesium 85 mg
niacin 2 mg
vitamin B6 0.56 mg
vitamin E 2.36 mg
167 calories

Motion sickness. If even the thought of traveling by boat, airplane, or by any form of transport which has a constant rocking motion, makes you feel queasy, then a fresh ginger juice may provide the solution. (One teaspoon of dried ginger in apple juice works well, if you are on the move.) SEE ALSO **peach fizz**

quantum leap

Said to be more effective than anything you can get in a drugstore, ginger is ideal for quelling nausea. Drink just before traveling.

Makes about ⅓ cup

8 oz apple
1 inch cube fresh ginger
  root, roughly chopped

Juice the apple and ginger and serve in a glass over ice. Decorate with some chopped mint, if liked. This drink can be diluted with sparkling mineral water to taste.

┌──────────────────────────────┐
│ **NUTRITIONAL VALUES** │
│ vitamin C 16 mg │
│ **160 calories** │
└──────────────────────────────┘

Stomach ulcers. These are caused by excess acid and the digestive enzyme pepsin and are aggravated by stress, smoking and acidic food and drinks. They can be controlled by keeping your intake as alkaline as possible, but if you have severe abdominal pain, you must always consult a doctor. SEE ALSO **red rocket**

well
healed

Both carrot and cabbage juices are renowned for having a healing effect on stomach ulcers.

Makes about ¾ cup

8 oz carrot
8 oz green cabbage

Juice the vegetables and serve in a tall glass over ice.

NUTRITIONAL VALUES
vitamin A 70,654 iu
vitamin C 105 mg
selenium 5 mcg
zinc 0.95 mg
180 calories

Diarrhea. Whether you're suffering from food poisoning, stress, travel sickness or jet-lag, diarrhea will dehydrate your system. This means you must ensure that your body gets plenty of liquids to replace the nutrients lost.

SEE ALSO **purple passion**

belly berry

Blueberries contain anthocyanosides, which are lethal to the bacteria that can cause diarrhea. **Makes ¾ cup**

8 oz apple
4 oz blueberries, fresh
   or frozen

Juice the apple, then whizz in a blender with the blueberries. Serve in a tumbler.

NUTRITIONAL VALUES
vitamin A 8,946 iu
vitamin C 20 mg
magnesium 18.5 mg
210 calories

Constipation. A sluggish digestive system, caused by poor diet and lack of digestive enzymes, can cause constipation, an uncomfortable affliction which may lead to blockage and distension of the bowel. A combination of fruit and vegetables high in fiber and cleansing properties will help to exercise and stimulate the abdomen and improve digestion. SEE ALSO **magnificent 7, easy does it**

way to go

This really could be called a lethal weapon–a dose of three potent laxatives that will get you back on line. **Makes about ¾ cup**

8 oz pear
1 oz pitted prunes
4 oz spinach

Juice all the ingredients and serve in a glass over ice cubes. Decorate with pear slices, if liked.

NUTRITIONAL VALUES
vitamin A 8,946 iu
vitamin C 80 mg
potassium 1,311 mg
302 calories

GOOD FOR **IBS (irritable bowel syndrome).** This may be caused by stress, so it is important to juice foods which help to reduce stress levels as well as dealing with inflammation. Avoid foods such as wheat, coffee, potatoes, corn, onion, cheese and white wine. A detox may prove beneficial. SEE ALSO **spring clean**

red rocket

Carrot and apple contain pectin, tannic acid and malic acid, which regulate bowel movement and soothe intestinal walls. Cabbage detoxifies the stomach and upper colon and improves the digestion.

Makes about ¾ cup

6 oz carrot
8 oz apple
4 oz red cabbage

Juice all the ingredients, including the apple core. Serve over ice in a tall glass and decorate with slivers of red cabbage, if liked.

NUTRITIONAL VALUES
vitamin A 49,523 iu
vitamin C 70 mg
potassium 1,159 mg
selenium 3.79 mcg
250 calories

GOOD FOR **Hangovers**. If you're paying the penalty for the fun of the night before, then juicing is probably the quickest way to detox your system. The "hungover" feeling is caused mainly by dehydration, and replacing lost fluids is the quickest way to help your body recover. Drinking equal amounts of juices and water ought to do the trick.

morning after

Papaya helps to calm the digestive system; cucumber flushes out toxins and orange gives a great boost of vitamin C. The overall effect is calming and rehydrating. **Makes about ¾ cup**

4 oz papaya
2 oranges
4 oz cucumber

Peel the papaya and the oranges (leaving as much of the pith as possible) and wash the cucumber. Juice them together and serve in a tall glass over ice. Decorate with slices of cucumber and papaya, if liked.

NUTRITIONAL VALUES
vitamin A 1,123 iu
vitamin C 218 mg
magnesium 51 mg
potassium 1,004 mg
selenium 2 mcg
184 calories

SORTING OUT YOUR SYSTEM

Osteoporosis. This debilitating disease primarily affects women who have gone through the menopause. It is imperative that even younger women supplement their eating plan with bone-strengthening foods. SEE ALSO **root 66**

sticks and stones

Turnip-top leaves contain more calcium than milk. Broccoli is ideal too, as it also contains calcium and folic acid. Dandelion leaves are excellent sources of magnesium, which helps the body utilize the calcium for healthy bones and teeth. **Makes about ¾ cup**

4 oz turnips, including the tops
4 oz carrot
4 oz broccoli
handful of dandelion leaves
6 oz apple

Scrub the turnips and carrot. Juice all the ingredients and whizz in a blender with a couple of ice cubes. Serve in a tall glass decorated with dandelion leaves, if liked.

NUTRITIONAL VALUES
vitamin A 50,391 iu
vitamin C 223 mg
magnesium 108 mg
calcium 398 mg
folic acid 210 mg
196 calories

GOOD FOR

Arthritis. The most common form of arthritis, whereby the smooth layer of cartilage that covers and cushions the ends of the bones gradually breaks down, mainly affects elderly people. The swollen and inflamed joints that result are an extremely painful condition. There are many foods that can ease the discomfort of this condition including cabbage, citrus fruits, berries, and fruits high in vitamin C. SEE ALSO magnificent 7

twister

The salicylic acid in grapefruit works to break down uric acid deposits and the carrot and spinach help to rebuild and regenerate cartilage and joints.

Makes about ¾ cup

4 oz pink grapefruit
4 oz carrot
4 oz spinach

Peel the grapefruit, keeping as much of the pith as possible. Juice all the ingredients and serve in a tumbler. Decorate with slices of grapefruit, if liked.

NUTRITIONAL VALUES
vitamin A 43,864 iu
vitamin C 167 mg
cysteine 43 mg
185 calories

GOOD FOR

Hair and nails. While there is nothing you can actually do to improve the appearance and texture of your hair and nails, as these cells are already dead, there is plenty you can do to their underlying, unseen parts: the roots. Root vegetables are high in potassium, so add lots of these to your juicer for a healthy head of hair!

SEE ALSO earth mother

hard as nails

This juice is high in potassium. **Makes about ¾ cup**

6 oz parsnip
6 oz green bell pepper
3½ oz watercress
6 oz cucumber

Juice the ingredients together and serve over ice with a sprinkling of mint.

NUTRITIONAL VALUES
vitamin A 6,331 iu
vitamin C 242 mg
potassium 1,400 mg
211 calories

Skin eruptions and acne. Potatoes are great for juicing as they aid your nutritional intake in several ways, particularly by providing vitamin C, along with the carrots in this recipe. Radishes are ideal for detoxification and prevent viral infections, colds and mucus. SEE ALSO **cool down**

hot potato

This juice contains potassium, phosphorus and chlorine, all good for skin eruptions.

Makes about ¾ cup

3⅓ oz potato
3½ oz radish
3½ oz carrot
3½ oz cucumber

Juice the ingredients together and whizz in a blender with 2 ice cubes. Serve in a tall glass decorated with radish slices, if liked.

NUTRITIONAL VALUES
vitamin 56 mg
potassium 1242 mg
chlorine 920 mg
155 calories

GOOD FOR

Skin disorders. There are many causes of skin disorders, ranging from stress to food allergies and vitamin deficiency. As the body's largest organ, your skin is the barometer of your body's health, being the first part to show any imbalances. It is also the first part to show the results of cleansing your system.

SEE ALSO **magnificent 7, red rocket**

herbi-four

All four ingredients in this juice contain bioflavonoids, which reduce inflammation. **Makes about ¾ cup**

6 oz red bell pepper
6 oz tomatoes
3½ oz white cabbage
1 tablespoon chopped parsley

Juice the pepper, tomatoes and cabbage. Pour into a tall glass, stir in the parsley and decorate with a lime wedge, if liked.

NUTRITIONAL VALUES
vitamin A 4,062 iu
vitamin C 264 mg
selenium 21.3 mcg
zinc 1.14 mg
120 calories

Eyesight. Remember when your mother nagged you to eat your carrots, so that you could see in the dark? Well, she was right, as carrots contain high levels of beta-carotene and vitamin E, which are necessary for maintaining healthy eyes. Chicory is helpful in preventing cataracts. SEE ALSO **twister**

vision
impeccable

This combination of vegetables provides a high vitamin A content that nourishes the optic nerve. **Makes about ¾ cup**

6 oz carrot
4 oz chicory
4 oz celery

Juice the carrot, chicory and celery. Whizz in a blender with a couple of ice cubes and serve decorated with lemon slices and some chopped parsley, if liked.

NUTRITIONAL VALUES
vitamin A 53,687 iu
vitamin C 33 mg
potassium 1,499 mg
128 calories

LOOKING GOOD, FEELING BETTER

Pregnancy care. Eating (or juicing) for two may seem overwhelming when you are first pregnant, but you do not need to double your intake of nutrients and vitamins, although it is recommended that you increase several of them. Nutritionists advise that, for most women, an additional 200 calories per day is all that's required, therefore juicing is a great way to increase your intake of nutrients while controlling your calorie count. More importantly, though, ensure that you eat (or juice) foods high in folic acid, to reduce the possibility of spina bifida. SEE ALSO **cool down**

earth mother

This juice is rich in folic acid and vitamin A, which are essential for fetal development and guard against pre-eclampsia.

Makes about ¾ cup

4 oz carrot
4 oz lettuce
4 oz parsnip
4 oz cantaloupe melon

Juice the carrot, lettuce and parsnip with the flesh of the melon. Serve in a tall glass with wedges of melon, if liked.

NUTRITIONAL VALUES
vitamin A 42,136 iu
vitamin C 115 mg
folic acid 93.75 mcg
204 calories

GOOD FOR

Morning sickness. One of the downsides of being pregnant is morning sickness. Ginger is an excellent stomach-settler–try adding a small amount to your favorite juice. Honey also helps settle a queasy stomach.
SEE ALSO **quantum leap**

peach fizz

Peach has an alkalizing effect on the digestive system, and ginger works wonders for nausea. **Makes about ¾ cup**

8 oz peach
1 inch cube fresh ginger
root, roughly chopped
sparkling mineral water
mint leaves

Juice the peach and ginger and serve in a tall glass over ice, with a splash of sparkling water and a couple of mint leaves. Sip slowly to calm your stomach.

NUTRITIONAL VALUES
vitamin C 10 mg
potassium 390 mg
127 calories

101

Immune system. All the juices in this book will benefit your immune system, as it is this which lets your body fight and prevent disease. Juicing is the ideal way to increase your energy levels. SEE ALSO chili queen

ginger zinger

A juice rich in antioxidants. The lime encourages the elimination of toxins.

Makes about ¾ cup

4 oz carrot
8 oz cantaloupe melon
1 lime
1 inch cube fresh ginger
 root, roughly chopped

Juice the carrot, melon, lime and ginger. Serve in a glass over ice. Decorate with lime wedges and seeds from a cardamom pod, if liked.

NUTRITIONAL VALUES
vitamin A 4,262 iu
vitamin C 137 mg
selenium 2.7 mcg
zinc 0.84 mg
166 calories

Immune system. The best antioxidants are found in citrus fruits, strawberries, kiwi fruits, raspberries and blueberries. This drink may help prevent or treat urinary infections, provide the fiber necessary to ward off colon cancer and aid weight loss as these fruits are all low in calories. SEE ALSO **frisky sour, morning after**

"c" breeze

A sharp clean-tasting drink full of vitamin A and vitamin C, selenium and zinc. **Makes about ¾ cup**

5 oz grapefruit
2 oz kiwi fruit
6 oz pineapple
2 oz frozen raspberries
2 oz frozen cranberries

Juice the grapefruit, kiwi and pineapple. Whizz in a blender with the frozen berries. Decorate with raspberries, if liked, and serve with straws.

NUTRITIONAL VALUES
vitamin A 693 iu
vitamin C 179 mg
selenium 4.3 mg
zinc 1.43 mg
247 calories

Nutritious food, fast. It's not recommended that you substitute juice for all your meals, but this recipe and Magnificent 7 on the opposite page are both very good if you're on the run. SEE ALSO **passion thriller**

green dream

This juice is packed with vitamin B3, niacin and folic acid. **Makes about ¾ cup**

8 oz apple
2 oz celery
2 oz kiwi fruit
½ lemon
3½ oz avocado

Juice the apple, celery, kiwi fruit and lemon. Transfer to a blender with the avocado and whizz for 20 seconds. Decorate with kiwi slices, if liked.

NUTRITIONAL VALUES
vitamin C 161 mg
vitamin E 2.89 mg
niacin 2.42 mg
folic acid 72 mg
347 calories

magnificent 7

We would run out of paper listing the nutritional aspects of this juice.
A great all-round energy booster. **Makes about ¾ cup**

3 oz carrot
2 oz green bell pepper
1 oz spinach
1 oz onion
2 oz celery
3 oz cucumber
2 oz tomato
sea salt and pepper

Juice the ingredients and season
with sea salt and pepper. If liked,
decorate with tomato quarters.

NUTRITIONAL VALUES
vitamin A 28,009 iu
vitamin C 105 mg
iron 2.41 mg
potassium 1065 mg
selenium 2.5 mg
zinc 0.8 mg
115 calories

GOOD FOR

Detoxifying. Watermelon is the ideal detoxifier; the flesh is packed with beta-carotene and vitamin C. Watermelon juice is so delicious that it's not a chore to drink a glass of this every day. By adding strawberries, you'll be receiving a great boost of vitamin C as well as helping your body fight against the bacteria in your system.

SEE ALSO **flush-a-bye-baby**

juicy lucy

High in zinc and potassium, two great eliminators.

Makes about ¾ cup

7 oz watermelon
7 oz strawberries

Juice the fruit and whizz in a blender with a couple of ice cubes. Serve decorated with mint leaves and whole or sliced strawberries, if liked.

NUTRITIONAL VALUES
vitamin A 6,562 iu
vitamin C 195 mg
potassium 950 mg
zinc 0.58 mg
130 calories

Detoxifying. Most people have heard of the cabbage soup diet but many don't know why cabbage is such a good detoxifier. As it aids digestion and prevents fluid retention and constipation, its benefits are noticed almost immediately. It is perfect for juicing as its nutrients are most abundant when it is raw. In fact, many nutritionists call cabbage the perfect food. Celery, watercress and pears are the ideal accompaniments as they also contribute to the detoxification process. SEE ALSO **red rocket**

spring clean

The cabbage and the pear rid the colon of waste matter and the celery purifies the lymph. **Makes about ¾ cup**

8 oz pear
4 oz cabbage
2 oz celery
1 oz watercress

Juice all the ingredients and serve over ice, decorated with celery sticks, if liked.

NUTRITIONAL VALUES
vitamin C 97 mg
potassium 1,129 mg
magnesium 48 mg
206 calories

| GOOD FOR |

Dieting. Dieting usually leads to water loss, not weight loss. By eating a sensible, balanced diet and exercising regularly, you will lose weight more gradually but it will be more likely to stay off. An excellent way to kick-start any weight-loss plan is through a one- to three-day juice detox, which will stimulate your system and energize your intentions! SEE ALSO **evergreen**

ginger spice

Drink a glass of this juice before a light lunch to maintain energy and banish the dieting blues. **Makes about ¾ cup**

10 oz carrot
2 oz fennel
3 oz celery
1 inch cube fresh ginger root, roughly chopped
1 tablespoon spirulina (optional)

Juice the ingredients and serve over ice. If liked, decorate with strips of fennel and fennel fronds. You can also add 1 tablespoon of spirulina, which contains phenylalanine, to suppress your appetite.

NUTRITIONAL VALUES
vitamin A 84,600 iu
vitamin C 43 mg
potassium 1,627 mg
magnesium 80 mg
183 calories

113

GOOD FOR **Dieting.** An advantage of following a juice plan at the start of your weight-loss program is that juices tend to be quite filling, which means you are less likely to reach for a bar of chocolate. SEE ALSO six pack, kale and hearty

green peace

An ultra green juice that helps to maintain energy levels.

Makes about ¾ cup

3½ oz broccoli
3½ oz kale
1 oz parsley
7 oz apple
2 oz celery

Juice all the ingredients and serve in a glass over ice. Decorate with kale, if liked.

NUTRITIONAL VALUES
vitamin A 10,574 iu
vitamin C 365 mg
selenium 5.14 mg
zinc 1 mg
228 calories

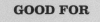

GOOD FOR

Weight gain. This is a really flavorsome drink and absolutely packed with calories. SEE ALSO **bugsy banana, green dream, passion thriller**

sweet chariot

This juice is full of complex carbohydrates that will help you gain weight if it is taken as a supplement to a normal balanced diet.

Makes about 1¾ cups

3½ oz pineapple
3½ oz grapes
3½ oz orange
3½ oz apple
3½ oz mango
3½ oz banana

Juice the pineapple, grapes, orange and apple. Whizz in a blender with the mango, banana and a couple of ice cubes for a super sweet smoothie. Serve decorated with orange wedges and mint.

NUTRITIONAL VALUES
vitamin A 4,631 iu
vitamin C 121 mg
selenium 3.3 mcg
383 calories

Children. The drinks from this page through to the end of the book have been designed for children. Juices are the quickest and easiest way to make sure your kids not only receive vital nutrients, but also enjoy their food at the same time. Juicing is so easy that you can ask your child to do it—this way they'll feel more involved.

bugsy banana

Full of iron, calcium, and potassium, this is an all-round booster that is great for bones and teeth and keeping colds at bay.

Makes about ¾ cup

5 oz carrot
3½ oz orange
3½ oz banana
1 dried apricot

Juice the carrot and orange. Whizz in a blender with the banana, apricot and some ice cubes. Decorate with chunks of banana, if liked.

NUTRITIONAL VALUES
vitamin A 44,570 iu
vitamin C 88 mg
calcium 101 mg
potassium 1,475 mg
iron 2.5 mg
204 calories

119

super shakey

A sweet dairy-free milk shake that aids digestion and is full of protein, calcium and vitamin C.

Makes about ¾ cup

8 oz pineapple
3½ oz parsnip
3½ oz carrot
5 tablespoons soy milk

Juice the pineapple, parsnip and carrot. Whizz in a blender with the soy milk and a couple of ice cubes. Decorate with pineapple wedges, if liked.

NUTRITIONAL VALUES
vitamin C 65 mg
calcium 80 mg
protein 6 g
266 calories

strawberry sunrise

This juice has a high vitamin C content to ward off colds. Strawberries are natural painkillers.

Makes about ¾ cup

7 oz strawberries
7 oz orange

Juice the strawberries and orange. Serve straight over ice, or blend with a couple of ice cubes for a thicker drink. Decorate with whole strawberries, if liked.

NUTRITIONAL VALUES
vitamin C 219 mg
potassium 694 mg
calcium 108 mg
154 calories

tummy tickler

Add a couple of juiced prunes if your child is
constipated. **Makes about ¾ cup**

10 oz apple
7 oz blackcurrants

Juice the fruit and serve over ice for a
great blackcurrant cordial substitute.
Decorate with extra blackcurrants, if liked.

NUTRITIONAL VALUES
vitamin C 415 mg
calcium 30 mg
300 calories

maybe baby

This is a highly nutritious, natural baby food.

Makes about ½ cup

4 oz pear

3 oz avocado

Juice the pear and blend with the avocado.

NUTRITIONAL VALUES
vitamin C 12 mg
218 calories

glossary

Aloe vera A supplement derived from a fleshy plant which can be added to juices. It has immunity-boosting, antiviral and antiseptic properties, and can benefit joint problems and irritable bowel syndrome.

Antioxidant A beneficial substance that rids the body of free radicals. Many vitamins, including A, C and E, are antioxidants.

Apiin A glycoside which adds a slightly bitter taste to foods.

Ascorbic acid Vitamin C.

Assimilation The process of digesting and absorbing nutrients into the body.

Beta-carotene (pro-vitamin A) A nutrient found in all dark green, orange or red fruits and vegetables that is converted into vitamin A in the body. It is an antioxidant and offers protection against cancers.

Bromelain An enzyme present in pineapple, which is effective in treating blood clots which may lead to thrombosis.

Calcium A mineral needed to ensure healthy bones and teeth, including the prevention of osteoporosis.

Calciferol Vitamin D.

Carcinogen Any substance that can cause cancers in the body.

Centrifugal juicer A widely used design that works by centrifugal force. Fruits and vegetables are fed into a rapidly spinning grater which separates the pulp from the juice.

Cholesterol A fatty substance found in most body tissues, including the blood, which can build up on the insides of blood vessels and cause blockages.

Citrus juicer A simple lemon squeezer used for juicing citrus fruits only.

Cobalamin Vitamin B12.

Collagen An elastic protein which forms connective tissue in the body.

Colon The lower and largest part of the intestine.

Degenerative condition A serious ailment that worsens over time.

Detoxification The process of clearing the body of a build-up of toxins, which could be contributing to ill health. The results are clearer skin, more regular bowels, more efficient kidney and liver function, and reduced stress, hormone imbalances and other inflammatory conditions.

Dithiolthiones The phytochemicals that speed up the action of the enzymes involved in the body's detoxification.

Diuretic A substance that causes you to pass urine more often.

DNA Deoxyribonucleic acid, the material found in body cells that carries genetic information.

Ellagic acid A phytonutrient which may deplete cancer-causing substances in the body.

Enzyme A substance responsible for the digestion and absorption of food into the body. Enzymes also convert foods into body tissue and raise energy levels.

Folic acid A nutrient found in green leafy vegetables, liver, pulses and wholemeal cereals that helps to prevent spinal disabilities in unborn children.

Free radicals Highly reactive molecules that damage cells, contributing to wrinkles, sagging skin, loss of muscle tone, age spots and the onset of age-related diseases.

Fructose An easily assimilated sugar found in fruits and honey.

Glucose A simple sugar found in many fruits and vegetables which is

quickly digested to provide energy.

Glutathiones Molecules found in the body which can destroy toxins such as carcinogens.

Holistic A treatment that works on the whole person rather than just their symptoms, to bring about complete good health.

Immune system The body system, made up mainly of antibodies and white blood cells, that works to resist infection.

Inulin A simple sugar that is converted into levulose by the enzyme inutase, making it safe for diabetics.

Inutase The enzyme that converts inulin into levulose in the body.

iu International unit, a standard quantity of a vitamin.

Levulose A form of fructose.

Lycopene An antioxidant which lowers the risk of cancer and heart disease. It is also responsible for protecting joints, muscles and brain cells.

Masticating juicer A juicer that works by pulverizing fruit and vegetables and pushing them through a wire mesh with immense force. This process extracts a large amount of juice.

Metabolism The chemical processes that occur in the body and result in energy production and growth.

mcg Microgram, one-millionth of a gram. A unit used to measure quantities of vitamins and nutrients.

mg Milligram, one-thousanth of a gram. A unit used to measure quantities of vitamins and nutrients.

Nervous system The body's network of specialized cells, including the brain, which transmit nerve impulses around the body.

Oxidization The breakdown of substances, including some vitamins and other nutrients, on exposure to air. Fresh juices should be drunk soon after they are made to ensure they contain as many nutrients as possible.

Pantothenic acid Vitamin B5.

Papain An enzyme which helps to break down protein in the body.

Pectin A nutrient found in the pith and cellular membranes of fruits which helps lower blood cholesterol levels.

Phytochemicals/phyto nutrients Plant chemicals which seem to prevent serious diseases such as cancer, heart disease, asthma, and arthritis. These chemicals

are at the forefront of research into food and health.

Pulp The fibrous residue left after juicing fruits and vegetables.

Pyridoxine Vitamin B6.

RDA Recommended daily allowance, the quantity of a nutrient needed each day to maintain good health.

Retinol Vitamin A.

Remedial treatment plan A plan of treatment designed to cure an illness or aspect of ill-health.

Riboflavin Vitamin B2.

Spirulina An extract of blue-green algae that can be added to juices to increase their levels of phosphorus, potassium, sodium, vitamin B3 and beta-carotene. Its main benefits are cell regeneration and renewal; it is also antifungal and antibacterial.

Supplement A substance such as spirulina or aloe vera which is added to a juice as a concentrated source of vitamins and minerals.

Thiamine Vitamin B1.

Tocopherol Vitamin E.

Uric acid A crystalline acid, a waste product eliminated from the body in urine.

Vitamin An organic compound essential, in

small amounts, to maintain normal health and development.

Vitamin A (retinol) An organic compound found in liver, oily fish and milk that keeps the eyes healthy.

Vitamin B1 (thiamine) An organic compound used in the production of energy and the maintenance of the nervous system, found in meat, milk, wholegrain cereals, dried fruits, nuts and pulses.

Vitamin B2 (riboflavin) An organic compound which helps the body derive energy from food and maintains healthy eyes, hair and nails. It is found in milk, liver, kidneys, cheese and fortified breakfast cereals.

Vitamin B5 (pantothenic acid) An organic compound known as the anti-stress vitamin, that boosts the metabolism and helps the body derive energy from food. It is found in liver, kidneys, yeast, wheatgerm, pulses and vegetables.

Vitamin B6 (pyridoxine) An organic compound found in meat, bananas, pulses, whole-wheat bread and rice, which balances hormonal change in women and helps cell production.

Vitamin B12 (cobalamin) An organic compound which aids red blood cell production and the maintenance of a healthy nervous system. It is found in liver, kidneys, oily

fish, meat, eggs, dairy products and fortified cereals.

Vitamin C (ascorbic acid) An organic compound found in most fruits and vegetables, particularly oranges, blackcurrants and kiwi fruits, that helps protect against cancers and coronary heart disease. It is an antioxidant and also maintains healthy bones, teeth and gums.

Vitamin D (calciferol) An organic compound which promotes a healthy nervous system and helps in the formation of bones and teeth. It is found in oily fish, dairy products and eggs.

Vitamin E (tocopherol) An antioxidant, organic compound which protects cells from free-radical damage and prevents against heart disease and cancer. It is found in vegetable oil, wheatgerm, nuts, oily fish, eggs, avocado and spinach.

Vitamin K An organic compound found in green vegetables (such as broccoli, spinach, cabbage and kelp), liver and tomatoes that is necessary in the formation of blood clots.

Wheatgrass A plant grown from wheat berries that is rich in chlorophyll and an ideal energizer when added to juices.

index

acknowledgments

The author and publisher would like to thank
Raw Health Ltd, 79 Myddleton Road, London, N22 8NE
for the loan of the Oscar Pulverizing Juicer.
www.goraw.com

Photography © Octopus Publishing Group
Limited/Stephen Conroy.

Executive Editor: Nicola Hill
Editorial Assistant: Jennifer Barr
Executive Art Editor: Mark Stevens
Designer: Joanna MacGregor
Picture Library Assistant: Taura Riley
Photographer: Stephen Conroy
Home Economist: David Morgan
Stylist: Angela Swaffield
Production Controller: Nigel Reed